She Believed She Could

So God Did

Christine Merino

I am thankful to God for always being there
and never leaving me, and for my parents and
friends who have supported me
and loved me.

To the memory of my parents
in gratitude for raising me as a Christian and
teaching me to have the strength and courage
to believe in myself.

Abuse is when someone causes us harm or distress.
It can take many forms, ranging from disrespect to
causing someone physical or mental pain.

A portion of our proceeds go to help women and children
who are victims of domestic abuse.

For readers ages 14 and up: Due to the content and nature of domestic violence, adult language is used to portray real events as they occurred. This is intentional, to avoid downplaying the abuse and to preserve the integrity of its seriousness.

Copyright © 2026 Christine Merino
All rights reserved. Except as permitted under the U.S. Copyright Act of 1976, no part of this publication may be reproduced, distributed, or transmitted in any form or by any means, or stored in a database or retrieval system, without the prior written permission of the publisher.

PSALM 111:1

Chicago, IL

Printed in the United States of America
First Edition: January 2026

ISBN Paperback: 979-8-218-90618-4

Library of Congress Control Number: 2026900021

Scripture references in this book were retrieved from Biblegateway. com
Amplified Bible, Classic Edition (AMPC)
Copyright © 1954, 1958, 1962, 1964, 1965, 1987 by The Lockman Foundation
English Standard Version (ESV)
The ESV® Bible (The Holy Bible, English Standard Version®), © 2001 by Crossway, a publishing ministry of Good News Publishers. ESV Text Edition: 2025.
New International Version (NIV)
Holy Bible, New International Version®, NIV® Copyright ©1973, 1978, 1984, 2011 by Biblica, Inc.® Used by permission. All rights reserved worldwide.
New King James Version (NKJV)
Scripture taken from the New King James Version®. Copyright © 1982 by Thomas Nelson. Used by permission. All rights reserved.
New Living Translation (NLT)
Holy Bible, New Living Translation, copyright © 1996, 2004, 2015 by Tyndale House Foundation. Used by permission of Tyndale House Publishers, Inc., Carol Stream, Illinois 60188. All rights reserved.

This book is designed to provide information in regard to the subject matter covered. It is sold with the understanding that the publisher and author are not engaged in rendering therapeutic, legal, or other professional services. If expert assistance is required, the services of a competent professional should be sought. Therefore this book should be used only as a general guide and not as the ultimate source of information on overcoming domestic abuse. The author and publisher shall have neither liability nor responsibility to any person or entity with respect to any loss or damage caused, or alleged to be caused, directly or indirectly by the information contained in this book. Any names in the book have been changed to protect individual privacy.

Table of Contents

CHAPTER 1 THE BIG PICTURE 1

CHAPTER 2 A NEED TO PLEASE 7

CHAPTER 3 LOVE AND BETRAYAL 29

CHAPTER 4 SEARCHING FOR SECURITY 41

CHAPTER 5 A RUDE AWAKENING 63

CHAPTER 6 TAKING THE HIGH ROAD 79

Chapter 1

The Big Picture

Iron sharpens iron,
so one person sharpens another.
(Proverbs 27:17, NIV)

This book is the story of my own experiences with domestic abuse, and it mirrors the stories of many women I've talked with over the years. We are united in our struggle against a justice system that is run by men and turns a blind eye to the real torture and trauma endured by many women who are abused, even after they are successful in leaving their abusers.

A female attorney I admire had excellent advice: "You cannot control what other people say and do. However, you can control how you react to it. You can also control how you let it affect you. The way you react and how you let it affect you molds you as a person. Be fierce."

So, how do we get to that place of inner confidence and self-empowerment after living through the hell of physical, emotional, verbal, financial, sexual, or psychological abuse? Of course, it's a process, a journey of peaks and valleys. But the most important things we can do along the way are to speak up and to support each other.

So often, a woman or girl who is abused tries to hide it out of shame. She might hope that if she just sticks it out a little longer, she can figure out how to change it, fix it, make it better. She might believe that she will lose too much if she leaves, that she needs to have a partner because being alone is much worse. She might worry that she will lose her friends or alienate family members if she leaves or if she speaks up about it. And if she tries to take a stand in the relationship, the abuse could escalate.

I was that girl and then I was that woman. And I have met too many others who have shared that pain, confusion, and overwhelming self-doubt with me. So many women who finally got free have discovered that abusers can always find ways to continue the abuse especially if there are children involved.

Co-parenting with an abusive ex is too often a continuing source of torment because the justice system so often holds back from enforcing its own rules and decrees until the evidence is undeniable and overwhelming. By then, even more damage has been done to the abused woman and especially to the children who are caught in the crossfire, and the enforcement of the decrees is too often mild and ineffective.

This book expresses my hope that women and girls trapped in abusive relationships can spot the warning signs sooner, that their friends and family members will understand and support them in freeing themselves and their children, and that the justice system will improve its oversight and effectiveness in identifying and pursuing proven abusers before they are allowed to inflict such far-reaching damage.

An important part of my story in this book is the role my faith played in seeing me through the toughest times. I haven't held back from describing those times but I'm so grateful that I can look at them now, knowing that I have been liberated from the anger and hurt.

God has brought me to a place of forgiveness and strength at last after all these years, and I will include Scripture verses that have helped me, hoping they might help you, too.

Another big part of my own healing and self-empowerment has been working with support organizations here in my state that work to raise awareness, as well as helping raise funds to support local shelters and nonprofits working to protect abused women and children.

The healing process could look different for any of us, but if we share as openly as we can with others and bring pressure to bear on our elected officials to stand up for the rights of women and children, we could help save not only each other but the next generation of young women.

For nothing is hidden that shall not be made manifest, nor is anything secret that will not be known and come to light.
(Luke 8:17, ESV)

I walked with Christine during her difficult journey, during which she gifted herself peace of mind. The precious gift of knowing she didn't lose her inner goodness; she freed herself.

—Diane T., Friend and Mentor

Chapter 2

A Need to Please

The lines have fallen for me in pleasant places;
yes, I have a good heritage.
(Psalm 16:6, AMPC)

I came here with my family from the Philippines when I was a baby. It was 1974. I don't remember the Philippines at all, but I have a lot of stories from my parents. They told me they had to leave because of martial law.

My mom told me she was frightened by the changes going on in their country. When the unrest there made many want to flee for their safety, my brother was 12 and my mother was pregnant with me.

My parents were more fortunate than most who were trying to immigrate to the U.S. because only professional people could enter this country easily at that time. My parents were educated accountants who were able to come here legally since the U.S. administration was welcoming CPAs from other countries.

When we moved to the U.S., we had a small apartment, and I remember being horrified by cockroaches when I was very little. It was in the Bucktown neighborhood of Chicago, a neighborhood that was quite different in 1974. Today, it's beautiful and built-up, but back then, there were drug dealers and prostitutes on street corners, and I remember when our TV was stolen.

It wasn't all bad, though. We had a happy, stable home. My parents were respectful of each other and hardworking. They were both thankful that they were able to come to the United States and they were adjusting to this new life, eager to become Americans without losing their cultural heritage.

My mom and I were close and I was always proud of her poise and professionalism as a businesswoman. To me, she was an intelligent, strong woman. She could be feisty and passionate, too.

My dad was always kind and respectful to her, and of my two parents, she had a little temper on her. She would throw plates at the floor sometimes if she got angry enough.

Her influence as a dedicated professional was an important part of my identity later as a businesswoman. She used to tell me, "I didn't raise a stupid girl."

And I understood from a young age what she expected from me. But there were other influences in my family life at home that affected me, especially in the way I related to men.

Even though my dad was a steady and calm presence in our home, he was strict, especially with my brother. We moved to Oak Lawn where my parents bought their first home. I lived in that Oak Lawn home from kindergarten until I graduated high school.

Moving to our new home was an easy and happy transition for me, but my brother was 12 years older, and it was harder for him to acclimate. We were one of very few Asian families in our new suburb, and with the Vietnam

War drawing to a close, I think my brother had a harder time than I did.

For me, Oak Lawn was a wonderful place, and I had a healthy childhood with my friends. My brother on the other hand, was a little more angry, a little more rebellious, and therefore had a harder time growing up, I think. When we were in the city before we moved to Oak Lawn, he got into a lot of fights in high school. I truly believe that stayed with him more when we moved to the suburbs.

My brother also had a hard time with our parents. More is expected of you when you grow up in an Asian family. Our parents were very strict – they were good parents, but they were new immigrants here, fearful, and they wanted to raise us well. They expected good grades and good behavior.

But my brother was more of a rebel as a teenager. My dad didn't take to that well. They had arguments, and consequences were threatened. I went to my room and shut the door whenever things started to heat up between them. I was determined never to make my parents get upset or worry about me like that.

Although my parents were always good to me, I had to get good grades to make them proud. I didn't want to go down the hard road like my brother, and that influenced a lot of my decision-making as I got older.

You either rise or fall under this Asian parental regime. My parents were young when they had my brother, so they were harder on him. I was the baby, so I got away with more. My brother had to babysit me a lot since he was 12 years older.

A lot of his insecurities and attitudes impressed themselves on me, and I learned quickly that pleasing other people would bring about the best results, keep me in my parents' good graces, and keep my brother appeased.

My brother was never physical in the way he picked on me. It was more verbal, always teasing and poking fun. He thought it was cute to call me Mutt Face and Flat Nose, but I didn't like it. I was one of only four Asian students at my school in Oak Lawn, and although the kids at school were welcoming, I felt different, I looked different, and I wanted to acclimate.

So, I dreamed about being the all American girl next door. The last thing I wanted was for anyone to call me names like Flat Nose. I became very conscious of my nose, an Asian Filipino nose. I tried to ignore the hurt but it stayed with me and became something I wished I could change in order to be more accepted.

But, bottom line, he was a good brother, and he never did anything to hurt me beyond teasing. I think in my heart, it was his insecurity because he didn't have our parents' approval. And no matter what nationality a family is, the older kid gets the brunt of most of the negative discipline and unreasonable expectations.

You know the old Chinese proverb: "You put your demons on your children." I think my brother did the best he could trying to fit into American culture.

I wasn't perfect, but I tried so hard to be "a good girl" just trying to find my way through high school. The pressure of trying to be perfect for my parents wasn't easy to process along with all the other challenges a growing teenager faces: the peer pressure, the struggle to be popular and accepted, and all the hormones kicking in.

I still had braces on when I made the big switch from our small junior high to a huge high school. It felt like the whole world opened up. New boys, new girls, the first taste of freedom and independence. It was intoxicating and exciting.

By the time I was a sophomore, I was watching many of the girls I admired pairing up with guys. Some would whisper secrets about no longer being a virgin and I started to wonder if anyone would end up liking me.

In my world full of Caucasian boys, would any of them decide to ask me out? I couldn't wait to get my braces off!

It seemed that all my friends were just as excited, scared, and hyper-focused on boys as I was. It was all we ever talked about. Who likes who? Who's going out with who?

Of course now I understand that we were all insecure and not sure if we felt good about ourselves or not. We were waiting for our first kiss, first love, believing that having a boyfriend would make everything much, much better.

My first romantic experience was when I was a sophomore in high school. I fell into a relationship that proved very difficult. My first boyfriend was John. He was tall and blonde, and looked a little like Vanilla Ice. He dressed like a surfer sometimes, and like a dancer other times.

At first, it was simple and fun. We were young and we were attracted to each other. He liked me, I liked him. We were both sophomores, and in my mind, my wish had come true. Despite the braces that were still on my teeth, somebody really liked me, for me.

John would walk to my parents' house at first, and though I thought he was cute and attentive in all the right ways, my parents didn't like him. They didn't like the idea of me being around any boys at all. So we would sneak going to the mall or to a movie or a dance.

My parents didn't want me having anything to do with a boy, and they insisted on knowing what I was doing at all times and who I would be with. Now as a parent, I know why. Did I listen at the time? No

But I did get involved with John, and over the next year or so, we became increasingly more physical. Once we had sex, I became very bonded to him and I believed that I loved him. He grew more and more possessive and jealous, and I was confused when he would shove me in anger if he thought I was being too nice to any other guy.

When I told him I didn't like that, he said, "Well, I'm not abusing you. I didn't punch you!" And he would make excuses, saying he loved me and he never meant to hurt me. And I would accept that because I didn't want to lose him and I wanted to believe that he loved me.

He was also jealous of the time I spent with my girlfriends and would show up to see if I was flirting with other guys or just to know what I was doing. It was like he wanted to own me.

Looking back, I wish someone would have stepped in to warn me early on that things were just going to go from bad to worse and I needed to get away from him. I wonder if I would have listened, because at the time, I was enamored of him and was so proud to have my first boyfriend, as if that somehow validated me.

I unfortunately felt I didn't have a voice of my own and now that I look back, I was so innocent and naive. What 15-year-old has a good idea of who they are and what they want in life?

But I was determined to make the best of it and endured things I shouldn't have. I wish I hadn't. If this is your situation, please believe me when I say that you need to get away and save yourself from the damage that will happen to you if you don't.

But unfortunately, I discovered that this kind of behavior from teenage boyfriends was common. Two of my girlfriends were having the same kind of experiences. So even though I didn't grow up seeing women treated this way in my household, I learned that my situation was not unusual, and that made it even harder for me to see a better way at that time.

I did have a few girlfriends who were adamant that I get away from John, and those mixed messages from my peers just added to my indecisiveness. Plus I knew my parents would not stand for my continuing to be with him if they knew the truth.

So, I struggled with what to do and tried to figure out a way to make the relationship work better. Clearly confused, insecure, and frightened. I really wish I'd known someone who could have shared words of wisdom from scripture with me. Maybe I would have listened.

Despite my fighting back about the abuse, John would insist that I was crazy and that I deserved to be shoved when I disrespected him. He'd say things like, "That guy flirted with you and you flirted right back!" when I knew that I had done nothing at all.

I have since learned that abusive men are often insecure, weak men who make themselves feel stronger by terrorizing women. I didn't put that together until I got older, but he was clearly the most insecure boy in his group of friends.

In high school, being involved sexually was like being brainwashed into joining a secret club or something. You want so badly to be independent, someone who is accepted, someone who can act like an adult, yet not quite an adult, and somehow believe that this was just the price you paid to be admitted to some Cool Kids club.

I decided the best thing to do was stay silent, because I didn't want to be kicked out of "the club." I needed to believe that I loved him and that I could hold my own.

The very first time I came home with bruises on my body, my mom lost her mind and swore at me in Tagalog and English, telling me to get away from this boy. "Are you crazy? What the hell are you thinking?!" she would shout. And my dad was very angry, too.

But for some reason, I couldn't turn my back on John. I honestly think it was only because he was my first sexual experience. I was afraid to be alone. John's ultimatums, manipulations, and lies had some powerful hold over me.

I had abandonment issues with my mom, too. She would take the long flight to the Philippines for family events like funerals and weddings and would stay a month at a time, and she wouldn't even tell me she was going until the night before, because I would get so upset.

Since John had such a strong hold on me with all his crazy jealousy, I mistook that for love and devotion. I was clearly in denial, so much so that I would pretend that the abuse wasn't as bad as it really was.

So, I hid my shame and put my best game face on. Auto-pilot, scared, quiet, and silent. You never think this will happen to you, even when it does.

But things escalated physically. He would slap me and kick me. I remember one time vividly. I was at my girlfriend's house and he was driving his parents' van around looking for me. I still remember to this day his parents' license plate number on that tan Dodge Caravan.

I was so fearful of him following me. I didn't know it at the time, but now that I suffer from PTSD, those scars still haunt me today.

When he found me that day outside my friend's house, he pulled over and leaped out of the car to grab me, yelling at me and making a scene. His two friends stepped out of the van and just stood there glancing around with their hands in their pockets. My girlfriend Samantha stood frozen on her front step, watching John in disbelief.

When he threw me down on the lawn and started kicking me, Samantha started screaming. I looked to his friends for help, but they wouldn't meet my eyes. It was as if the whole world was frozen, too. No one was going to help me.

I managed to roll away from him and ran into Samantha's house with her. We locked the door behind us. It was frightening. We hid in the house, hoping he and his friends wouldn't try to come in. Samantha wanted to call the cops but I just held my sides, wincing from the pain, and shook my head.

The sad thing is, I was afraid to call the police. At the time I thought I loved him, but I didn't. I didn't even love myself at that point. I wanted so much to be in love, but now I realize I didn't know what love was.

I wish I would have read 1 Corinthians Chapter 13 over and over back then. It could have saved me a lot of pain and heartache to know what love really is.

When I go to counseling now as an adult, what happened to me that day is the vision that stays with me. Counselors would ask, "What would you do for that little girl?"

I tell them I would go back in time and hug her and save her! I would tell her to know her worth, that she is the prize, and she doesn't have to give herself to anyone until she finds that very special person who treats her the way she deserves, and who deserves her love in return…And I would kick the shit out of any pussy of a man who would do such a thing!!!

I want to save that girl. That's why I'm writing this book.

I remember another vivid memory, getting back to the Mutt Face name-calling I endured from my brother. My dad knew that my feelings about my nose really affected me.

It may sound dumb or vain to somebody who doesn't know what that's like, but when you're not this Caucasian, blonde-haired, blue-eyed, beautiful girl next door, and you're wanting so much to fit in, things like that weigh on you. So, when my dad asked, "What do you want for high school graduation?" I said I wanted a nose job.

The sad thing is, not long after that, I went back to John. I was obviously not secure with myself. I stayed with this sadistic jerk for all the wrong reasons.

One of those reasons was because I felt I had the right to make my own choices. You tend to do that when you're 17. Since my parents were telling me to stay away from him, I wanted to make up my own mind.

Note to self, when parents tell their teenage child "No," it often makes that child even more likely to do it. How true the words from Proverbs are: Foolishness is bound in the heart of a child. Every parent knows this!

One day a few weeks before graduation, John picked me up in his parents' van. I made the mistake of telling him that I was going to get a nose job for my graduation. His outraged reaction was instantaneous.

He shouted, "You're going to end up looking like Michael Jackson!" and before I could get away, he beat me up right there in the car. It was so traumatic.

He beat me so badly that day, that when I went to the plastic surgeon's office later that week to discuss the procedure, the doctor asked my dad, "What happened to her?"

My dad was livid about it. Rightfully so. He had been yelling at me, telling me to get away from this boy, but I was the idiot staying with this guy because I had such low self-esteem.

I didn't have low self-esteem all the time, but there was something about John that kept me coming back to him. It was simply my emotional attachment to my first sexual partner – nothing else. It wasn't about his appearance or personality or anything.

The plastic surgeon said, "If this happens again, I'll call the cops."

I was trying my best to avoid John, but he always followed me. It was a small suburban town, and there were only a few places teens would go. I drove to a burrito place in my parents' car with one of my girlfriends next to me in the front seat.

As soon as I parked, John pulled up with that ugly Dodge Caravan once again and just climbed right into the back seat.

"Get out!" I said emphatically. "I don't want to be with you anymore."

He just sat there, looking at me with a smug look on his face. My girlfriend threatened to call the cops and John just laughed.

Still afraid of him, I somehow had the courage to say to my friend, "No, just get out of the car, I'll take care of it." I stayed in the driver's seat and as soon as my friend closed the door, John reached over and slapped the side of my face. I covered my face with my hands, trying to figure out what to do to get him out of the car.

Just at that moment, a cop drove by, slowed his car, and rolled down his window. Thank God!

"Ma'am, are you okay?" he asked. His eyes were full of concern and suspicion. I saw John retreat into the back seat, glowering at me threateningly.

I was both terrified and angry, but I managed to say loudly and clearly, "No, I'm not!"

And so the cop pulled him out of the back seat, handcuffed him, and took him away in his squad car. That was the last time I saw John face to face. I went to the police department and filed a restraining order.

I have been able to forget everything else about John and block him out of my memory except for those specific events. I'm still amazed that I put up with his abuse for so long. That first sexual experience is a huge turning point, and it can sometimes be confusing, almost like being brainwashed into thinking that it's some form of true love.

Clearly, mine was not! Adults talk about first crushes and young love as if they are frivolous or unimportant. But to a teenager, it often feels like your first taste of independence, and therefore keeping that first physical relationship going can seem more important than anything else.

In therapy, it was helpful to bring up all these memories and truly try to deal with them, even though the flashbacks are still tough to relive. It's not only important to work on dealing with the trauma and abuse, but most importantly to learn how to forgive yourself.

The only way to let go of all the trauma and truly start to heal is to learn how to forgive yourself. Forgive yourself for allowing it all to happen and most of all, uncover the reasons why and how. Harboring pain and anger only keeps the PTSD going.

Years later, John tried to reach out through Facebook to apologize. I responded with a simple "Thank you." I didn't want any contact with him, period. He tried to friend me, but I declined and blocked him.

It was good to receive his apology, but any further contact wasn't necessary or useful to either of us. Those years are best forgotten. I wanted to continue to move on, with God's promised help.

Fear not, for I am with you;
Be not dismayed, for I am your God.
I will strengthen you, Yes, I will help you,
I will uphold you with My righteous right hand.
(Isaiah 41:10 NKJV)

CHRISTINE MERINO

The purpose of our spiritual gifts is to put Jesus Christ on display! Christine is constantly readily available to connect with others through her words, her writing, and her actions. Her genuine interest to help strengthen believers' faith enables her to create wonderful opportunities to encourage faith with others. I praise God for all his glory!
—Alma C., Colleague

Chapter 3

Love and Betrayal

Then I met Tee, the love of my life, so I thought. He was just so hot! He looked like Johnny Depp pre-cocaine, like 21 Jump Street Johnny. That bad boy, pretty boy, and don't-give-a-fuck boy, attracted me and I was mesmerized. It was lust, really.

He was 18 and I was 17. I even remember what I was wearing the first time I saw him. A pair of Express jean shorts and a white Express shirt – so 1990. We were at a juice bar called Crazy Rock, a club where you could go under 21, which was a lot of fun. I had a curfew, but I was allowed to go out with my girlfriends until 11:30.

When I saw Tee for the first time, we took a long look at each other. One of those looks like in the movies and I can honestly say my heart stopped. My braces were off and I felt pretty for the first time in a long time. It felt like a movie! Time stood still and he came up to me and talked to me and that was it – I fell in love with him.

Tee, I honestly can say now, is who I consider to be my very first love. He was my friend. I guess you can say we really "grew up together" from that point forward. Then we got married at 23.

My whole world revolved around him. If he said I looked good in silver jewelry, I wore silver jewelry. When he said I had naturally pretty ankles, I was ecstatic. If he said, "I like your hair long," I kept it long, and I've always had long hair ever since. As you can tell, he had become my everything.

I was so happy leaving the awful relationship with asshole John and coming to this new relationship. Tee wasn't hitting me and he was good to me. He did get jealous though, if a guy or his friends paid attention to me, but he never hit me.

He never verbally hurt me either. He was just fun and goofy and we laughed together. I loved him at first out of lust and attraction, then I genuinely loved him in that intense way that only happens with your first true love.

I did notice that he had a lot of girlfriends though before he met me and before we got seriously involved. Of course he did – he was beautiful! I somehow convinced myself that he only loved me. He was a player, but like so many other young women, I was certain I could be that one girl who would change him. And how many girls are still thinking that way today?

After six years of dating, I gave him an ultimatum. I said, "We either get married or I'm done." I shouldn't have done that, because when we got married, he wasn't done being a flirt.

Tee's mom was a volunteer at the rectory of his church. A sad event happened before I met Tee. His mother had cancer and something tragic happened near the end of her life. She fell down while on her volunteer shift and no one at the church saw her fall or realized she was there until hours later. By then she had passed away.

The priest at that church counseled us before our marriage and told me personally that he would marry us, but he felt that Tee was carrying anger against God and the church and he felt Tee was not a good choice for a husband.

Looking back, I wish I would have listened to the priest, but I was way too in love. If I could go back and talk with my younger self, I would say, "Listen to your elders and pay attention to the warning signs." And I would repeat some wisdom from this scripture:

> ***Those who listen to instruction will prosper;***
> ***those who trust the Lord will be joyful.***
> ***(Proverbs 16:20, NLT)***

But I only had my relationship with John to compare to, and to me, Tee was obviously the better choice because he didn't hit me or verbally abuse me. So, I thought it was a step up in the right direction.

We were married and I was with him all the time. In my heart of hearts, John was nothing. I blocked him out for good reason. John would even circle around Tee's house at first when he knew I was there, blaring his music and revving his engine in a threatening manner. He was such a jerk but he finally gave up.

I didn't know better at the time, but my relationship with Tee did not have a healthy balance, because I was doing everything he wanted. I was crazy in love and trying to do everything to please him. If I had an opinion that didn't agree with his, as soon as he complained about it, I would let it go, just to avoid having any fights.

Looking back, I know that I had no idea who I was yet, and once again was completely focused on making sure he stayed with me, no matter what. It didn't occur to me how unhealthy this was.

Tee and I moved into our own house, thanks to a down payment (i.e. wedding gift) from my parents. I was positive that we were the happily-ever-after couple. He was a stockbroker, and I was working at a doctor's office in the finance department.

I wanted to go to med school, but I didn't apply, because I didn't want to be that busy and miss out on time with Tee. That was a big mistake. Once we were married, he was always out golfing all day every Saturday and most Sundays anyway.

My whole life circled around work, Tee golfing with his dad, and then we would do something together Saturday night and/or Sunday. Our first year of marriage was wonderful and exciting.

But then, he started to stay away from home for longer periods of time after work because he said we were "having problems." But we weren't really having problems; we were just settling into the relationship.

Tee appeared to be losing interest in the marriage but I refused to see that. He was making good money as a broker at that time. There were a lot of drugs and girls around him, but I was completely unaware.

I remember him saying to me, "I want to go to my dad's house. I just have to think about some things."

I asked, "What do you have to think about?"

He said, "I don't know."

Obviously, I didn't have a good feeling about that and started to worry. On July 4th, 1998, I told my brother, "Let me take your car. I'm going to follow Tee."

So, I took my brother's car and I sat outside my father-in-law's house for hours. Along came Tee driving this girl, someone I'd never seen before. He was in the driver's seat and there they were, making out.

My heart was pounding so hard as I got out of my brother's car. Tee looked up and gasped, and I could see him saying, "Oh my God!"

When he got out of the car, the girl jumped into the driver's seat, locked the door, and drove away. I hauled off and slapped Tee as hard as I could.

"You just broke my spirit!" I yelled at him. I honestly don't know where those words came from, but it was true. They just exploded out of me.

He tried to pin the blame on me, saying I wasn't good for him anymore or something. But I stopped him right there.

"Don't you even try that. This isn't my fault."

I found out about the girl he was kissing in the car. She worked with him. She wasn't married but she knew he was married – but really in the end, that didn't matter. He was the cheater.

I told him, "I don't want to babysit you for the rest of your life. This is in the Ten Commandments – adultery."

But I still loved him. I was devastated. I was working at a hospital at the time, I stopped going to work and was in a fetal position most of the day and night. I was so depressed that my neighbors were concerned about me. I was blaring Enya so loud just begging God to make it stop, all with the dire reality that I was now alone in the house that we once built.

I felt betrayed and shattered. The cups we used, the furniture we picked out, the bed that we used to make love in, were all there as idle reminders of a love now lost. I never realized how broken I could get, how totally miserable.

I would sit for hours crying, not eating, sleeping and just trying to talk to anyone and everyone, really whoever would just listen, about the pure devastation that I felt. The loss, the death of a relationship, the pain and the sorrow…I just wanted it all to go away.

I felt as if my best friend who I grew up with had not only just died but so had my husband. It was like two different people in my head but obviously I knew he was the one person I needed to let go of and move on from, but nobody really gets that until they go through it.

After a time of grieving, I got a new job. I got back on my feet and refinanced the house. I know now that God was teaching me this:

I can do all this through him who gives me strength.
(Philippians 4:13, NIV)

My parents by the grace of God stood by me. Tee asked me one day to meet him at the swing set in a park where we used to go as teenagers.

He asked if we could get back together again, and I said, "No. I don't trust you. You see, the problem is I was loving you, and apparently you were loving you, but nobody was loving me! You don't deserve me."

He said, "Christine, if you ever need me, let me know."

"Need you for what?" I asked.

He said, "I don't know, for money or something?"

I was confused at first, and then taken aback. I shouted, "I don't even know if you realize this – I knew you when you had nothing. I don't care who you think you are right now. You're a fucking liar and a cheater, you broke my heart, and you don't deserve me! So take your money and get the fuck out of my life!"

That was Tee. I loved him when I divorced him. I was still in love with him, but I had to leave, if anything, for myself. I had to love myself. My best friend once said 20 years later,

"Christine you are a strong girl, stronger then you think, because I know you really loved Tee and yet you still left."

She was right. I loved Tee when I left him and I know if I can do that, I can do anything.

God is within her; she will not fall.
God will help her at break of day.
(Psalm 46:5, NIV)

And God will help you, too.

CHRISTINE MERINO

Christine is the ultimate girls' girl—always ready to lift others up. When I was going through a divorce similar to hers, I knew I had to reach out. She became my guide, my strength, and my inspiration for who I could be on the other side of it. I truly don't think I could have made it through a single day without her constant reminders that God had my back and was with me, too.

—Missy D., Friend

Chapter 4

Searching for Security

I didn't have kids with Tee. I was starting to do well on my own after the divorce. I got back on my feet and I was thankful for a simpler life being single. Tristan, a guy I knew from college, kept resurfacing in my life.

When he finished school, he called my parents' house and asked to speak with me. We had just hung out as friends when we were in school, but I knew he had always liked me. I thought he was a nice guy but he honestly wasn't my type.

After my divorce, he tried again. After two or three years of being in the friend zone, I started to give in a little. He always tried to talk me into something more, saying "Let's just date and see."

He asked me to go with him to a Cubs game on a Saturday and I agreed. We were already two years into being "just friends," so I thought, why not?

I was out with my friends the night before and had stayed out late since it was Friday night. Tristan called me that night and said he wanted to leave at 10 am for a 1 pm game.

"10 am?" I asked, surprised. I wasn't being rude, but I was calculating how much sleep I might get. He got mad at me on the phone because I was still out with my girlfriends, and hearing him freak out at me even before he took me out on our very first "date" should have been a red flag.

Now that I look back, I really should have paid more attention to that.

That's what sticks out in my head now about Tristan and how everything started – that Cubs game. We ended up going and were a little late. He was so hell-bent on getting there early, it was crazy.

I felt bad for disappointing him and apologized, even though I honestly didn't do anything wrong. He made me feel bad.

Looking back, that set the stage for a difficult and let's just say an unbalanced relationship, but yet again, I failed to see it.

Maybe I just didn't trust myself to pick wisely in the love game again. It felt safer to choose someone who seemed the complete opposite of what I had looked for before. Since he was not my type, I ended up saying to myself, well let's see where this goes.

I was not in love with him in the beginning, but I grew to love him in the marriage, as a friend. Anyone who had been as badly hurt, betrayed, lied to, and cheated on can probably understand what I am saying.

I vowed to never let anyone hurt me that badly ever again. Period. That's the truth. Once you are that hurt, you just try the best you can to put it behind you and move on.

But the pain never truly goes away.

We had fun at first. He was cool and book-smart. He was like Chandler Bing, Matthew Perry's character in *Friends* – all funny and happy-go-lucky on the outside. I asked Tristan why he had *so* many friends, because he always liked to hang out with so many people in large groups.

With Tee, it was usually just the two of us with an occasional friend here and there. But with Tristan, it was always 20, 30, 40 people. I asked him, "Are we still in high school?" but he just said he was comfortable that way. He said his parents were divorced and maybe that was why.

He told me he was the class clown and that was his way to get people to like him. But on the inside, at the house, he would yell and scream when something wasn't the way he wanted it. He managed to hide that side of himself very well during the lead-up to our marriage.

Of course, I know now that I never should have married this man just because he was the exact opposite of the other two guys and seemed a safer bet. When I told my parents, though, they were happy. They said the same thing; they wanted me as far away as possible from my past.

So I made a decision based only on my own understanding. I wish someone had shared this wisdom from Proverbs with me:

> *Trust in the Lord with all your heart,*
> *and lean not on your own understanding.*
> *(Proverbs 3:5, NIV)*

We had a conservative honeymoon. Tristan had never been out of the country, so we went to Europe. It was not luxurious, just simple and reasonable. He had to go get his passport for the first time.

It started out badly – Tristan got mad at me on the plane because he said he didn't like flying, but I didn't know if he was just tired at the time. Then it got worse. We were in Paris at a Burger King eating lunch, and he was yelling at me for something trivial. That was the first time he called me a bitch.

There was a guy sitting near us who said, "Sir, I don't know you, but you're clearly with a beautiful woman, your wife I assume, and I'm going to be honest with you, if I could only be as lucky as you." He said that to my husband of a week. So, the signs were all there, but now my path was set, so I decided to try making the best of it.

In the first part of our marriage, I learned quickly that if I just took care of things without complaining, didn't offer many contrary opinions, and gave him plenty of time to just laze around the house, things would go decently.

He was more of a homebody than I was and loved to just sit and watch movies. To this day, I don't watch a lot of TV because of this. Married life was far from perfect, but as long as I didn't trigger him, there was an uneasy peace.

But we had trouble getting pregnant. My uterus was inverted and I was having a hard time conceiving. Eventually, we had to go to the fertility doctor for intrauterine insemination (IUI) to get Tristan's sperm put inside me, which is very painful. The first three times were paid by our insurance, and the last two attempts were paid out of pocket.

While I was doing IUI, Tristan became psychotic, thinking that I was trying to avoid getting pregnant. It was hurtful and humiliating at the same time. I was faithfully doing the whole IUI procedure monthly, self-inducing shots to my own butt and thighs in addition to a lot of emotional and physical preparation.

So when he started checking my medicine cabinet thinking that I was trying to avoid getting pregnant, I was surprised and offended. There didn't seem to be an end to the things that upset him. I really tried to understand him, but I guess I never did.

Tristan became more and more convinced that I was trying to sabotage our efforts to get pregnant despite all the care I was taking to show up for all the shots and take every pill required. Everything is strictly scheduled to maximize the chances for pregnancy and I was very stressed about staying on top of it all.

It's about the farthest thing from romantic and much more taxing on a woman, not only physically but mentally and emotionally. Why would I go through all this pain while secretly trying to keep from getting pregnant?

It was then that I began to suspect that Tristan was a narcissist. I never could prepare myself in time for his mood swings and sudden rages. When this unwarranted paranoid behavior started, I began studying narcissism.

Tristan would tout himself as "so smart" so often that the girlfriend of one of his friends sarcastically referred to him as "all-knowing" when describing him out loud once, laughing to others. Yet you could tell by her undertone of sarcasm that she didn't like him. It was beginning to seem that others had started to catch on that he was conniving and manipulative.

He looked like a great guy to everyone outside the house, and that's what narcissists do. They want everybody to think they are perfect. But behind closed doors, it's a very different story.

Tristan was a control freak and paranoid, which are two hallmark characteristics of a narcissist. He brazenly checked my medicine cabinet regularly to see if I was taking the pills correctly and if I had any other pills in there that would keep me from getting pregnant.

It was ridiculous that he would accuse me of such a thing and tell his sister about his suspicions. That was a big fight. I was outraged, hurt, and so offended. Why was he like this?

After four failed attempts of IUI, on the fifth time, we succeeded and our daughter was conceived. Two years later, we were able to conceive naturally and brought our son into the world. What a joy it is to be a parent. Even a difficult marriage can't change that.

With the children in the picture, keeping the marriage alive became even more critically important to me. Being a mother of two young children comes with a new pile of stresses along with all the joys, and I found an even greater need for God in my life than ever before.

Tristan was a Baptist and I was Catholic when we started dating. Originally, he promised me that we would go to church together, and I was even willing to go to his church or a nondenominational church. Then, once we were married, he only wanted to go on major holidays.

Once we had kids, though, he said that fellowship was not important and he didn't have to go to church to be a Christian. I tried taking the kids to church a few times and then started listening to TV evangelists to try to fill the lack of spirituality in my life.

I still wanted to go to church, but he insisted that I didn't have to go to church to be a Christian. We went to a Baptist church a couple times, but then he didn't want to go. My kids and I would go to church on holidays, but he wouldn't go with us.

When I was little, I used to go with my parents on Saturdays at 5, so it was really important to me. I needed to hear the word of God. I was seeking God because I was so unhappy. This was the cry in my heart:

> *Create in me a pure heart, O God,*
> *and renew a steadfast spirit within me.*
> ***(Psalm 51:10, NIV)***

Maybe going to church and hearing the scriptures preached would have helped Tristan to be calmer and more reasonable. Maybe having God in his life would have opened his heart and given him more peace. But I couldn't get him to go.

Home life was getting harder despite my efforts to stay out of Tristan's way and make a nice life for all of us. I was working full-time, doing all the cooking, cleaning, shopping, driving the kids to their activities, and taking care of the house. But Tristan was becoming more and more contentious and critical. It felt like the more I did, the worse he got.

One of the memorable fights we had was about putting a frying pan into the dishwasher. It was dishwasher-safe, but because it was a new pan, he told me he wanted to take care of this pan and not put it in the dishwasher. In all my busyness, I forgot that part, and when I was home from a long day of work and cleaning up after dinner, I was distracted and accidentally put it in the dishwasher.

"You lazy bitch!" he yelled when he found out. "How dare you do that?"

Over a pan! I couldn't believe it!

Another time, I was cleaning up after dinner and he was watching *Annie* with the kids for the millionth time. They were little, around 8 and 6. From the living room, they could see me working in the kitchen.

Tristan had just bought new kitchen glasses and I was loading them into the dishwasher with the other dishes. I was exhausted from the day, and I broke a glass from the set of new glasses.

From the living room, he yelled a string of the worst obscenities at me right in front of the kids, including the words "you fucking lazy cunt!" while *Annie* continued to play. I was stunned and horrified. As a fair-minded person, I always felt that the punishment (or the criticism) should fit the crime. So his irrational reactions were always a shock to me.

Things were going very badly, but I stayed for the kids. He would throw and break things in the house when he lost his temper. There were times when my girlfriends saw past his nice-guy pretense. If I tried to let go a little and get away for a glass of wine and dinner with friends, they would point out that whenever I let loose and had a good time, they noticed Tristan would try to put me in my place and control me.

I knew they were right, but I felt helpless to change it. I guess I was still hoping he would begin to change back to the man who had been my friend years ago.

His big thing was words. He was verbally abusive and very controlling. It was emotionally draining to be with him. He would yell and scream, and I felt like I was walking on eggshells. On some days, I just tried to make everything fine and perfect to stop the fight, to keep the peace and hopefully have a decent weekend with the kids. But, if it didn't go his way, he would give me the silent treatment for days.

In my 17 years of marriage to Tristan, he was always this guy outside the house that he wasn't on the inside behind closed doors. He was lazy and angry inside. He would fall asleep on the couch and I'd leave him on the couch, because I didn't want him up in bed with me.

When he would lay next to me in bed, I'd be crying because I didn't want him near me. I would ask God, "Is this what you want for me? Is this all there is?" I would pray and cry. I wondered how many other women were trapped like this, but I certainly felt all alone. Praying was my only hope and comfort, the thing that kept me sane.

> ***Humble yourselves, therefore, under God's mighty hand,
> that he may lift you up in due time.***
> ***(1 Peter 5:6, NIV)***

I wish I could have viewed him as an unhappy person who needed some help. Dealing with his moods might have been easier that way, but I was too focused on how to protect myself from the abuse. I'd listen to music and pray and dream of my exit.

But I never cheated on Tristan. I never even emotionally cheated on him. I tried marital counseling with him, both together and separately. The therapists identified a need for anger management for Tristan and diagnosed me with ADD.

Tristan in defiance even asked, "Don't you think maybe I might be bipolar?"

The therapist said, "No, because with bipolar disorder, you can't control where and when you get angry, and it seems you do. You wait to get behind closed doors or wait until you two are alone, or at home, so no, it is clearly an anger management issue."

Later, our therapist recommended a divorce, as things had gone from bad to worse. Over the years, I saw several different therapists but none of them seemed to really click with me. They didn't offer true compassionate and wise feedback, but would just take notes and nod their heads and expect me to carry all the weight of the conversation.

What I needed was a close personal relationship with God. Though I felt Him there, in the midst of turmoil and a constant sense of dread, it was hard to stay close. Sometimes it was hard to believe He was really there when things got bad, but I knew I needed to hang on for dear life.

This verse was one of my lifelines during that time:

And we know that God causes everything to work together
for the good of those who love God
and are called according to his purpose for them.
(Romans 8:28, NLT)

My original relationships with men in my childhood came back to affect me again during a difficult time when my kids were still young. My mom died in 2007 and my dad passed in 2015. Before he died from cancer, my dad lived with us part-time for the last few years of his life. I shared the responsibility for caring for him with my brother and his family. At our house, Dad stayed in the walk-out basement.

Now Tristan couldn't hide his anger anymore because Dad lived with us. His good behavior could only go so far. Once my dad saw and heard firsthand how it was, he urged me to get out of the relationship.

The cancer had traveled to my dad's brain. Tristan said he didn't feel comfortable with my dad at our house because of that. He didn't think it was safe to have him there with the kids because my dad was starting to see people who weren't there.

Dad wasn't dangerous – he just started hallucinating because the cancer was in his brain. But since we had to do everything Tristan's way, I complied. I didn't agree with him, but I was tired of fighting him. So, my dad went to stay at my brother's house at the very end, even though I wanted him to keep staying with us.

Now that my brother felt he had to bear the brunt, my brother and I really had it out. When the nurses started going to my brother's house, he wouldn't let them in. I called my brother and asked why, and he started screaming and swearing at me. He said it was none of my business.

So, I went to his house, and he got in my face and told me, "I can't believe you, I don't care if Dad dies. This is not my responsibility. We were supposed to split it."

When he started to lunge at me again, I said, "Get in my face one more time and I swear to you, I'll call the cops."

Then my brother spit on me and swore at me with a string of curses in front of the deacon. The deacon was shocked and said, "What is wrong with your brother?"

My brother's kids were in their 20s at the time, and they ran upstairs. Everyone left me downstairs with my brother. His family was afraid of him.

I didn't care, because it was about my dad. It took me a long time to forgive my brother for the way he acted when Dad stayed with him. I know now that many people taking care of a terminally ill loved one suffer from burnout, and it makes them do and say things they normally wouldn't.

I have one sibling and I remember my mom saying that all we would have was each other. I can say now that I still love my brother. I'm thankful for the nice things he did for me when I was young, and I choose now to look past the teasing that was so hurtful at the time. I see him differently now. I have forgiven him and I wish him well.

I love this quote from C.S. Lewis: "To be a Christian means to forgive the inexcusable because God has forgiven the inexcusable in you."

Forgiveness is so important to God. It brings a feeling of release and emotional healing for the person who does the forgiving. Of course, it's hard to do and it can take a long time. It did for me, but my whole life changed for the better when I was finally able to do it. I leaned on the words of this scripture:

> ***For I can do everything through Christ,***
> ***who gives me strength.***
> ***(Philippians 4:13, NLT)***

When my dad died, I took some of the money he gave me and bought a condo. That was the beginning of my exit strategy as I began seriously contemplating what to do.

Things really came to a head with Tristan at last when he took a company car home and parked it in our garage, but he parked it under a shelf with a big, heavy stainless steel portable cooler teetering over the car.

I came home and parked on the other side and told him I didn't think parking the company car under that cooler was a good idea. He insisted it was fine. Toward early evening, the cooler fell on the company car. I told him, "I told you that wasn't a good idea. But the best thing to do is to take it to a body shop and get an estimate to fix it."

He asked me, "Can you do that for me?" I said I had to get to work the next day and it was his problem, but he kept at me, pestering and insisting that I take care of it. Like always, I finally gave in as I always did in the marriage and I said I would take it in.

I imagine he must have been pissed off and annoyed that he hadn't heeded my warning and I turned out to be right.

But things had started to change for me. I told him that if I was going to do this for him, I would do it my way. That was a new development in the dynamic between us. Before this, I had avoided direct confrontations with him due to his explosive temper.

These words really fit the change that was taking place in me:

> *Have I not commanded you? Be strong and courageous.*
> *Do not be afraid; do not be discouraged,*
> *for the Lord your God will be with you wherever you go.*
> *(Joshua 1:9, NIV)*

Then Tristan started dictating to me exactly how to get the estimate because he just had to be "in control." I stood my ground this time. I let him know that if he wanted to do it his way, he should do it himself.

We argued and bickered in our car about this, our voices getting louder and louder, in front of our children aged 10 and 8. We were on our way to what was supposed to be a family dinner at a nice local restaurant.

I was in the driver's seat and he yelled at me about how to fix his problem. Today, looking back, I can see that he was taken off guard by my unwillingness to give in. It must have been very threatening to him. I realize now that I should have stood up to him much earlier, rather than constantly silencing my own voice.

We got to the parking lot of the restaurant, and he completely lost his temper, jumped out of the car and slammed the door, throwing a tantrum, and screamed at me publicly for all to see.

He called me names and cursed at me in front of the restaurant and most importantly in front of our kids. He called me a fucking bitch and told me to shut the fuck up as he stormed away down the sidewalk, causing yet another spectacle.

I followed him in the car with the kids crying and yelling out the window for their dad to get back in the car. This was a totally disturbing and sad scene.

Now that I know better how to handle such destructive situations, I wish I would not have followed him. I could have stayed in the parking lot and calmed the children down. I could have explained that their dad needed time to walk off some of his anger.

Instead, though, I begged him to get back in the car to help quiet and calm our upset children and just stop the trauma. Something inside of me switched on, and I knew with my whole being that it was time to end the relationship.

I told him firmly, "This is crazy. You are crazy. This is terrible and unhealthy for the kids. I am done!" That was the lightbulb moment.

He tried to backtrack and get back in control, but I was ready. I told him that I had lost all respect for him. He tried every way he could to downplay his behavior, but I was finished giving him everything he wanted, doing everything his way, and putting up with the unhealthy toxicity of our home.

I was done being afraid.

I wanted to put all my energy into making a better way forward for myself and the kids. I realized that Tristan did not now, or likely might never, understand the way a husband is to love his wife:

> **For husbands, this means love your wives, just as Christ loved the church. He gave up his life for her.**
> **(Ephesians 5:25, NLT)**

I now understand the anger and desperation I felt in that moment, but there was also clarity born out of those feelings. Sometimes that's what it takes before we can make a move forward. I wish I could have had that clarity sooner, but I wasn't ready until that point.

"For I know the plans I have for you," declares the Lord,
"plans to prosper you and not to harm you,
plans to give you hope and a future."
(Jeremiah 29:11, NIV)

Chapter 5

A Rude Awakening

After all these experiences of abuse – physical, emotional, and verbal – in my life, I thought it would finally end when I got the courage to leave my husband. I was done, I was mentally exhausted, and I had to ultimately make the decision to protect myself and my kids. But I soon discovered that he could still abuse me and try to control me through our children.

Despite the court system that promises to enforce the rules of the divorce, in my state, my ex was still able to break the rules over and over. He made me out as a bad parent and called me names in front of the kids.

He called my own family and reached out to life-long old friends and badmouthed me to try and get them on his side. You figure the hard part is over when you finally decide to leave. But it rarely is. This was a level I didn't expect.

We had a court-appointed app to use for correspondence to protect the kids' rights and there were rules about how this communication could go. No swearing, no demeaning words, no slandering at each other's place of business. And there are fines in place for breaking those rules.

But over the course of time, Tristan managed to call me a Bitch over 50 times, Asshole 9, Cunt 1, a Piece of Shit 10, and told me to Fuck Off 8 times, just on the court-appointed app. Not to mention how often he used those and many other names on texts to me and in manipulative conversations with the kids.

I went to the trouble to count those in the app and report them to the court officials, yet no fines were ever issued to Tristan. They could easily see for themselves by checking the app, but all they did was send him a warning any time I reported violations.

The lawyers got a firsthand look at just how awful he was, but the shocker was that nothing much came of all that evidence of abuse. It seemed that they just processed the information away in the case, and at a certain point much later on after multiple documented abusive behaviors, they finally did come around in a later court case about his interference with my parenting time and made him sign a decree that he would stop name-calling. After that he would be fined if he did. But he never was fined.

Don't these people in authority understand that verbal abuse is just as damaging as physical abuse? They must have known it at some point, or these rules wouldn't have existed. So why do they so often do nothing when the rules are broken?

Our daughter was 10 and our son 8 when we finally split up, so all of that hostility, name-calling, and verbal violence had fallen on young, impressionable ears. With the state officials maintaining a non-involvement stance, my feeling of helplessness about that is one of the saddest aspects of my life.

Here is just one example of the kind of manipulation that occurred: When the kids were at Tristan's house, he would feed them the food they liked – processed foods, carryout, Starbucks, McDonald's, etc.

He kept all kinds of high-sodium, unhealthy snacks in his cupboard both for himself and for them. But because I am aware of his and my family's genetic tendencies toward heart disease, diabetes, and cancer, I often cooked real food for them.

He would tell the kids that I had "no food for them" because I didn't stock up on ramen and Pop-Tarts and get fast food delivered during Covid. He must have been so worried that the kids wouldn't love and respect him that he went to great lengths to make himself look good in their eyes.

I wanted them to have a balanced diet, but kids are kids and they wanted junk food. So of course they would complain about my efforts to make balanced meals for them and keep healthier snack choices on hand for them at my house. Divorced or not, this seems to be a common problem for most parents.

It only got worse during Covid when they had to shelter at home and attend school online. They ate mostly junk food and fast food at their father's. Nutritious meals and snacks at my house were criticized by him as unpleasant and unsatisfying because the kids didn't look forward to eating that way.

During contentious divorces, the court will appoint a Guardian Ad Litem (GAL), like a lawyer for the kids who mediates between them and the parents. Our appointed GAL was a young man who had no children and was not married. So he really didn't understand raising children or being married, but we had no choice about who was appointed to us.

So when the kids would complain that I didn't have food available that they could eat, it was a strike against me with the GAL.

This kind of uphill battle can be even harder without an attorney who is deeply committed. My attorney now is a female, and a powerful female. So, things are looking up as far as legal representation.

The justice system in post-divorce child cases is not fair. Even when you're divorced there can still be turmoil through the arrangements with the kids. The only people making money, in my opinion, are the attorneys.

You think you're trying to get justice and all the while the attorneys are just making money off you. Not only is it a lot of time wasted, it's pain, anger, and crying – time wasted I could have been spending with my kids.

How could a man you divorce be able to continue controlling you by controlling your children, riling up the system, and pushing the envelope with nonsense and noise? The court consistently refused to issue anything more than a warning each time, but according to Illinois law Sec. 10-5.5 regarding visitation obstruction:

> *When a parent is convicted of the offense, he or she receives a petty offense with a fine of up to $500 for the first two offenses. Subsequent offenses are class A misdemeanors that are punishable by up to one year in jail and a fine of up to $2,500.*

None of these penalties occurred and there were multiple instances of parenting time interference. He would return the kids to me later than the agreed time, which amounts to yet another form of manipulation, control, and disrespect that never seemed to stop.

This is classic behavior by narcissists to devalue their partners in order to get their own way and feel powerful. He belittled me constantly in front of others and especially in front of our kids.

Over two years ago, I wrote this to my lawyer. I wish I could tell you that things have gotten any better since then with the justice system, but they haven't:

> *Last week I took my ex to court because he emailed me an abusive hate email in recent months. I had all the proper documentation including proof of prior examples as well as supporting documentation showing*

he is not to communicate with me outside of the agreed-upon third party app. So in essence, he wasn't supposed to email me in the first place.

Despite all of the above, basically I was told "Divorce is civil" and that "Civil contempt cannot be punished."

*It's been 3 years! We're divorced! I left! I am just asking how much manipulation and continued abuse is one supposed to still take? When is enough **enough**??*

I just want to know when exactly does it go from being Civil to downright Harassment???

During the two years of Covid, one of my friends got locked into one of my bathrooms because I live in a 150-year-old farmhouse and the lock mechanisms were old. We had to call the police to come and break the top half of the door to get her out. I called a handyman to fix it and had to wait a long time for him to come.

In the meantime, I rigged up a sheet over the top half of the door to give people privacy in the bathroom, but Tristan made a big deal out of what a terrible mother I was not to have that door fixed right away and had the kids report that to the GAL.

It is unconscionable for someone to have so much disregard for the mental stress and pain he is causing for the children. When you finally get free, you think, "Now, life is going to be better. It's all going to be okay now!" Then the rude awakening hits.

As the ex-wife, you are now the enemy and your abuser draws battle lines, constantly portraying you as the problem. And that leaks into the kids' lives and puts them on edge, forcing them to take sides or dropping them without a safety net into a world of confusion and pain.

I had been praying to meet a kind Christian man who would go to church with me, and three years later, we found each other. When Tristan found out that I had met someone and started dating, he didn't like that my boyfriend was coming over when our kids were there. He kept the kids at his house and wouldn't let them come out to spend my rightful parenting time with me.

He came out to my car and was yelling at me in front of the kids who were in the house watching. The neighbors couldn't avoid hearing it. He wanted to know how I could be sure the man I was dating wasn't a child molester. He said he wouldn't allow his kids to be in danger. This put me in a bad light, frightened the kids, and worried the neighbors.

Around this time, Tristan put in an offer to buy a condo in the same building as the condo I received in the divorce. This condo was my refuge in the city for me to enjoy with my kids, though my house is near my work and the kids' school in the suburbs. For him to try to move into the same small condo building really upset me.

I was already feeling so fearful of the effect he was having on me. I was horrified when he boasted to me that he was planning to move into my building and laughingly said, "Don't worry if you see me in the building. We can be peaceful."

Right? How many thousands of condo buildings could he have chosen?

Things went from bad to worse. I was in my car in his driveway waiting for the kids to come out, and I wanted to get my golf clubs out of the garage of our old house.

"That's fine," Tristan said, but did not give them to me.

The garage door was open, so I told him that I was going to get my clubs. He was angry, as usual, about our differences in parenting the kids. He was yelling at me and I decided not to get out of the car.

"Why don't you just call your fucking lawyer and tell him about this?" he said as he grabbed the golf clubs and hurled them at the driver-side door of my car.

I sat there, horrified. That was certainly a high point in my PTSD feelings. All I could do was sit there and wait for the kids to come out. I wasn't going to exit that car for anything.

The most humiliating thing was that the kids were witnessing all of this through the front window and were terrified to come outside. The neighbors could all see this in broad daylight, but no one came out to try to stop him. I felt so alone and defenseless and outraged at the same time.

During our marriage, Tristan would often verbally abuse me, screaming and yelling in front of my own family and close friends. Before the divorce, they would say, "What on earth is wrong with him? You should leave him."

But when I finally did leave him, they seemed to forget that they had all agreed that I should. They seemed surprised that I actually did it. Maybe it was easier when we commiserated about our problems with our relationships and we were all suffering together with abuse, depression, and other things.

We numbed our pain together with laughter and mutual compassion, but when I left the marriage, it was astounding how many friends and family members didn't know what to do with me then. It was as if I had left a club or stopped playing a game, and they turned away from me.

It was so hurtful until I began to understand that they were still trapped and it was hard for them to relate to someone who got free. I must have presented too much of a challenge to them and they needed to establish distance from me. They weren't able to accept this change, that I was finally doing something better for myself. I guess misery truly likes company.

Tristan tried to abuse me by brainwashing the members of my family and ex-friends who didn't like the "new me" who got free. He called them to complain about me, and they commiserated with him about how much they didn't like who I was turning into. It was a crazy, mind-boggling pattern.

Tristan sent emails calling me a bitch to my company email address, which made them accessible to my professional colleagues. He sent messages like that on the parenting app, too, but they had nothing to do with the kids – the app was only for the purpose of communicating about the kids. It was endless.

He would tell my clients, who were old friends of ours, not to work with me anymore. He slandered me and my business in front of our kids, to our friends, to my clients, and on social media. It's shocking how much chaos and harm one angry person can cause.

But our divorce decree specifically says we are not to slander each other in front of the children, at our place of business, or in any way on social media. He actually used my picture twice in a slanderous social media post. I have never named him on social media or used his picture.

After I moved away from our house, which he got in the divorce, I moved to the next town over. My company's bookkeeping provider erroneously sent my W-2 to my old address after I moved. Tristan told my 12-year-old son to text me with this news: "I got your mother's W-2 and I shredded it. Now it's her problem."

Asking my son to send that text was inappropriate, manipulative, and cruel. Children should not be forced to act as go-betweens in a contentious divorce, but so often they are sucked into the drama, and the damage is done.

About five years after the divorce, I still struggled with his abusive behavior and his interference of my rightful parenting time. When I complained about it to my friends, some of them said, "It's been 5 years – get over it. It is what it is, and the kids will figure it out."

But what is a woman supposed to do when the abuse still continues! Five years later, and he was still breaking the visitation rules of our decree. It was an ongoing crime that was never punished.

Here was my answer to these friends who thought I should just let it go and get used to it:

> *Five years later and he is still interfering with my time with my kids. But in this state, what does that really mean? THIS is why I am loud about this stuff! Thousands of dollars, hundreds of hours. I am not going to stop fighting for my rights! This is abuse even after you leave the marriage. It's all wrong and it is a crime!*

There is a very draining series of steps required every time you try to stick up for your rights. The police require your appearance at the station, then you fill out a report, then they won't do anything about it but file it, and they tell you to take it to your lawyer. Then you have to go to court and pay attorney fees, and then the court is supposed to fine him or put him down as committing a misdemeanor. Neither of these penalties have ever happened.

At one point, they finally ruled that I would be given extra parenting time. But good luck with that, because it meant I would have to negotiate that with my ex. It was exhausting, and it felt like it would never end.

During this overwhelming time of frustration, I found much-needed strength in scriptures. Now that God has helped me forgive Tristan, I hope our children can benefit from the kinder interactions between their parents.

*Do not be anxious about anything, but in every situation,
by prayer and petition, with thanksgiving,
present your requests to God.
(Philippians 4:6, NIV)*

CHRISTINE MERINO

During my divorce, Christine was the support I could lean on, genuine and always present. She reminded me of my worth, and that real love and care exist. Through one of the most painful experiences of my life, she was always there helping me find my way back to myself, even sending me daily quotes or verses that helped me get through the hardest days. I'm truly thankful for having such a supportive and wonderful friend in my life. I love you and thank you for being there for me. I couldn't have imagined going through divorce without you.
—Michele S., Friend

Chapter 6

Taking the High Road

I divorced Tristan in June 2019. By the time Covid hit, I really felt the need to share my story with other women and try to help them not fall into the traps I fell into. I started a brand in 2021 because of the anger and the pain, and I decided to use the abusive terms in a positive and empowering way.

I felt all alone through what I went through, and I didn't want other women to feel isolated and helpless like that.

When I left the marriage, it was after 17 years plus two years of dating before we were married. All the while, I was going through a lot of verbal abuse and being controlled. I needed an outlet.

That outlet was to use the demeaning word which Tristan called me so often and turn it around into a statement of power instead of an insult.

I created this brand as a form of therapy in a time of frustration and outrage. It is called Badass Boss Bitch (BABB). I realize now that it's a very angry-sounding name, but anger is a necessary first step of getting free and finding your own way out of an abusive situation.

When you are trapped inside it and the thought of leaving scares or paralyzes you, the only thing strong enough to break you out at first is raw, powerful anger.

My therapy, my outlet, was to create this BABB brand to show other women, young and old, that you can leave – you don't have to take abuse. In my case, how could I give my own daughter the message that women shouldn't take abuse from a man if I was still taking it in my life? So, I had to leave the abuser for my sake as well as for hers.

I gained purpose in my pain and BABB became a passion. I created T-shirts, started a podcast, and trademarked it. I gave the profits from the proceeds to a local domestic violence shelter.

I did some online sales and tried to give back that way. I wanted to show my daughter and other beautiful young women that we can overcome and change something bad into something good.

As Gloria Steinem said, "The final stage of healing is using what happens to you to help other people. That is healing in itself."

Now, a few years later, I have processed more of the deep frustration and anger. Now I can see more clearly just how much I have been supported in my healing by a loving God.

I have trademarked a new brand that reflects where I am today. By the grace of God, I lived through all the years of confusion, betrayal, and desperation. The new brand is called She Believed She Could, So God Did (and it became the title of this book, too).

Now all glory to God, who is able, through his mighty power at work within us, to accomplish infinitely more than we might ask or think.
(Ephesians 3:20, NLT)

I'm sure other women have endured much worse abuse, and I know many are still trapped in these toxic relationships. But in my life I've survived by seeking God, the Word of God, and church.

> **_Praise the Lord! I will thank the Lord_**
> **_with all my heart as I meet with his godly people._**
> **_(Psalm 111:1, NLT)_**

The pain and the purpose to fight back was the reason for the BARB brand, but the overcoming of it all is expressed through this new brand. That's because I know God has always been with me. So it really wasn't me. God's always been there for me and enabled me to do all of it.

My goal is not just to tell my story. I want to join other women to help them empower themselves by sharing their stories. I have met many other women who have their own versions of this same story.

Whether it's physical, emotional, verbal, sexual – whatever abuse that women have endured, I really want to give back because I know I'm not the only one.

The state that I live in has not treated women in domestic violence situations fairly. We need to raise awareness and band together to change that, for the sake of the women and their children.

There are cases that just get paper-pushed and even though it appears to be the right thing for the courts to maintain impartiality, it seems like there's no justice. It's just 50/50. So often with abusive partners, it's just not that simple.

First and foremost, I want to offer two avenues for women to come together in small and large groups to openly share their challenges and strategies, but most of all to know that they are not alone.

The first avenue is through Badass Boss Bitch, when the pain and confusion are raw and real, when change is imminent. I really feel in my heart that this brand, BABB, is taking the pain of being called a bitch and empowering that word.

I've created this to make women aware that they don't need to stand down, and they are never alone. They have a voice and they can find help. That's what this brand means to me.

The second avenue is through She Believed She Could, So God Did, when enough healing and stabilization have taken place, allowing us to have a clearer vision for the road ahead.

We can help each other thrive and move forward. We can tap into the power of our spirituality and gratitude, and we can coach each other and be there for each other. Then we can support and guide our daughters, family members, and friends so they don't end up in the same situations.

A well-guided support group has incredible value for abused women. I think it's important to have a trained counselor there if possible, as well as women who have successfully navigated their exit from a toxic relationship. These survivors, like me, can share their battles and victories along the way.

The healing isn't easy and it isn't fast. It's a process that we can all help each other with. I want to be part of making groups like this available to more and more women.

Sometimes we just need to be reminded that we are strong, we are able, and we are powerful. We need that reassurance mentally, emotionally, spiritually, and financially to know that we are okay, and we have options and resources available.

When we are trapped in an abusive relationship, we are often in that hole of anger, sadness, helplessness, and depression. So often the abusers want us to feel like we are crazy, that the abuse is our fault, that we deserve it. We can be sucked into believing that we are unlovable and unreasonable.

And all the while, we have been tiptoeing around the abuser, trying to put out the fires, trying to keep the peace, trying to make everyone happy. But then, where are you after all that? Where am I?

There comes a time when we are depleted, when there is nothing left for us to go on. After years of trying to prevent bombs from going off in the house, trying so hard to make sure everyone is okay, of course it's going to take time to get your head clear and find your way.

When the abuser insists that we are making all this up, and they drag the children or other family members into that message, it's one of the most devastating aspects of the whole experience.

It's hard enough to finally leave the relationship and get free. But it's much, much harder to endure the negative opinions of our children, family members, and friends who are listening to the abuser's version of the story and then act distrustful or dismissive of us.

When these challenges come up, that's when an abused woman can really feel all alone. The emotional and physical impact of all that stress is toxic and taxing. These brands have been part of turning that pain into purpose for me. And now, it's my passion to give back to women, to show them that they can also overcome.

Life isn't just about money. For me, it's about leaving something behind, leaving future young women, our daughters, and ourselves the ability to know we can rise above and be powerful. We can be strong. We can be great. We don't have to put up with any pain or abuse at the hands of someone else.

I also encourage women to take advantage of therapy. I think it's very necessary to let it all out, because it gets poisonous when it's trapped inside. The control I was put under, the silent treatment, the raging, the screaming, the insults, and the constant demeaning – all of that is what I must heal from.

After seeing therapists at times throughout my marriage with Tristan, I finally found a female therapist after the divorce. A friend highly recommended her to me. I saw her several times and she helped me to establish better boundaries, coaching me to avoid feeding into the traps he was setting to upset me.

She explained that it's best to ignore a narcissist, which of course was hard to do when trying to get my parenting time.

My therapist was around my age, a gentle and steady person. She had been divorced too and had kids, so we shared a lot with each other about relationships with men and the challenges of parenting after divorce. She was personable and relatable, calming and sincere, as well as a very good listener, thorough, organized, and professional.

Her office was homey, comfortable, and inviting. and the people on her staff were very kind and helpful. There were calming colors all around me, with an atmosphere almost like a neighborhood coffeeshop where you could spend hours chatting.

I felt instantly relaxed just sitting in a chair in a cozy environment with lots of eye contact. It was like being with a wise and compassionate old friend. I would highly recommend searching for a female therapist first.

She didn't talk down to me, which I really appreciated. "I understand," she said. "Unfortunately this is not uncommon. Try not to react because that's what a narcissist wants. Focus on your kids and your healing with them, be present for your kids. Take your time. It does take quite a bit of work in therapy to overcome PTSD."

"PTSD? Isn't that what military people go through?" I asked.

"Yes. You have been traumatized for 17 or 18 years. You are having this recurring reaction to the ongoing traumatic situation that didn't let up, and it trains your body to tune itself to high stress levels. Even though you are divorced, because you are co-parenting, the stress source is still there and your body is still reverting back to the pain you felt when you were in the marriage. Over time, therapy teaches you and your body to turn a corner and make lasting change."

It wasn't easy to keep up the search for a therapist who could truly help me, but she was worth the wait because she really made a difference for me. She made me feel normal, and her diagnosis of PTSD really illuminated what was going on and gave me hope that I could conquer it.

In my life, I had been through physical, emotional, and verbal abuse. The verbal abuse to me was more painful. Physical abuse was certainly painful for me, but the verbal abuse left damage that is mental, emotional, and long-lasting. Those wounds can be more difficult to heal.

The turmoil becomes emotional, mental, and financial – it's like a perfect storm. And we all need shelter from the storm, with compassionate and caring people who understand what we're going through.

Along with help from my therapist, I have found another dimension to healing:

> ***Don't worry about anything;***
> ***instead, pray about everything.***
> ***Tell God what you need, and***
> ***thank him for all he has done.***
> ***(Philippians 4:6, NLT)***

If I could talk to the little girl inside me, I would say, I'm sorry I put you through that. I'm sorry that I allowed us to get hurt." That's what I would say to the young teenage girl who was being beat up by John.

I would pick that little girl up. I would make John stop, and then I would hug that little girl and show her how to get free and how to love herself.

Most importantly, one of the hardest things to do after living through abuse is to forgive yourself for submitting to it. I have been helped so much in therapy to work toward complete forgiveness of myself. That is when we are really free – when we understand, accept, and forgive ourselves.

Now I'm watching my own daughter and her friends who are about the same age I was. I don't want them to do what I did, forcing myself to just endure.

Nowadays girls have more of a choice. They don't have to stay silent; they don't have to be quiet. They have more opportunity and more freedom. They have more strong women behind them. That's what I want to help provide.

The toxicity of abuse is so often generational. The kids see it played out in their lives in the home for as long as the abused woman stays, and then they get to watch another version of the abuse if the woman leaves.

It's still about a man controlling a woman either way, but once the woman gets out, then she is portrayed as the enemy of the family. She is accused of being selfish and not caring for the kids anymore when she leaves the marriage. So often, the kids grow up to expect vengeful behavior in relationships and they often fall into it themselves.

That is why it's important to tell our stories. If we keep hiding the truth or downplaying it, if we don't fight back and call out these abusers to the authorities, we are just perpetuating this vicious generational cycle of abusers and victims.

I remind the young women in my life that they are smart, powerful, and beautiful. I remind them that beauty gets them in the door, but their brains keep them there. If we can empower a young woman, that's the ultimate goal. They're our future. You don't want your daughters or friends to marry a guy or be with a guy because they have to, even if they have kids.

I don't believe a woman should stay in any relationship if it's not healthy, because kids absorb everything. That's why the brands I've created have helped me as an outlet. They are my therapy now.

I talk to women for my business; my 9-5 job is insurance. Then I do real estate, too. I love helping women empower themselves. I love helping women realize they don't have to be just a partner and in the background. They can be the decision makers. That is very powerful for me.

Giving back to organizations that support women and children affected by domestic violence means a lot to me. There are so many ways to grow a business or an organization to a level where it can generate a profit to be donated. Social media, special events, holding seminars, podcasting, publishing articles and books, and creating support groups all contribute to building awareness of what you're doing with your business or organization.

I'm an advocate for women to fight for their rights despite all the ineffectiveness of the justice system. I've spent thousands of dollars in post-divorce fighting back and defending myself. Not everyone has the means to do that, but there are low-fee and no-fee legal entities that can help.

In my marriage I wasn't able to stand up for myself as much as I should have. But post-divorce, I can honestly say I have made it my passion. I won't accept being bullied and I won't let my voice be unheard. This is my Why now, turning passion into purpose and giving back.

The fact is that nothing gets done in court, just more and more forms filled out, and allowing abuse to continue, unless we push back. I found my strength and my passion in fighting for my own well-being as well as for my kids. And that passion now extends to any women who are shut down and isolated inside the trauma of abuse.

All of this strength and the ability to overcome is thanks to God. He has been there with me and for me the whole time. When you try to learn to love yourself and forgive yourself, that's a big step forward.

It's easy to be disappointed that you didn't stick up for yourself sooner, to feel helpless and angry, and to fall into self-destructive behaviors. But God has something better for you.

My brother's verbal abuse to me when I was a young child set the stage for a lifetime of accepting that kind of treatment. I went on from there to continue to put up with insults, acts of violence, and criticism from men as if that was just the way things are supposed to be.

I was used to being the underdog, and it's critical for the underdog to come out of the victim trap and find ways to be self-actualized, gain confidence, and forge a new life being empowered. I went through a very dark time of living inside the identity that my abusers created for me, and the road ahead requires me to step up and set myself free into the light.

I heard one woman say, "Don't be with somebody just because they love you. You have to be with someone because you love them, too." I loved my first husband so much and was hurt so badly when he cheated on me. I realized I then opted for a relationship that didn't have love so I wouldn't get hurt as deeply.

The real relationship is the one you have with yourself. If you really love yourself, you don't need to settle for being with someone who doesn't truly love you.

And if you love God, his power, strength, and passion will flow through you. And he will give you more than you need to handle the troubles of life.

Each of you should use whatever gift you have received to serve others, as faithful stewards of God's grace in its various forms.
(1 Peter 4:10, NIV)

CHRISTINE MERINO

Be still, and know that I am God.
(Psalm 46:10, ESV)

Not only that, but we rejoice in our sufferings,
knowing that suffering produces endurance,
and endurance produces character,
and character produces hope,
and hope does not put us to shame,
because God's love has been poured into our hearts
through the Holy Spirit who has been given to us.
(Romans 5:3-5, ESV)

CHRISTINE MERINO

Restore to me the joy of your salvation,
and grant me a willing spirit to sustain me.
(Psalm 51:12, NIV)

*She is clothed with strength and dignity,
and she laughs without fear of the future.
(Proverbs 31:25, NLT)*

Blessed is she who has believed that the Lord would fulfill his promises to her! (Luke 1:45, NIV)

www.ingramcontent.com/pod-product-compliance
Lightning Source LLC
Chambersburg PA
CBHW061453040426
42450CB00007B/1334